Middle-East | Asia | America

Middle-East			Asia			America			
			c36 000 Primitive people in Lower Yellow River Valley	30 000 B.C. people hunted.		c25 000 – 17 000 B.C. Hunting people inhabit Canada, Mexico, Andes			c50 000 – 20 000 B.C. First migrants from Asia reached North America
Phoenicians	Sumerians	Hebrews	Chinese	Japanese	Indians	Mayas	Aztecs	Incas	First Americans

Time	Phoenicians	Sumerians	Hebrews	Chinese	Japanese	Indians	Mayas	Aztecs	Incas	First Americans
4500			First pottery							
3000		Oldest inscribed tablet at Kish								
2800	Phoenicians settle									
2500		Ur supreme				Civilisation in the Indus valley				
2000	Egyptian, Babylonian, Hittite influence	Hammurabi of Babylon rules	Semi-nomadic / Abraham, Isaac and Jacob	Hsia Dynasty						Pottery in south-east of North America
1700			Egypt dominates	Shang Dynasty		Aryans invade				Eskimo culture begins to use sea as a source of food
1500	Phoenicians trading in Mediterranean	First Assyrian Empire								
1000			King David Israel & Judah	Chou Period				Culture in Mexico		'Mound Builders' inhabit Ohio Valley
1000	Carthage established		Assyrians Babylonians					Climax of Oltec culture		
500	Persians dominate	Wars between Persians and Greeks	Greeks	Civil wars	Yao period begins	Greeks reach India		First pyramids in Mexico		
500	Greeks take Tyre		Romans take Judea	Ch'in Dynasty / Han Dynasty		Greeks expelled				
0 B.C./A.D.	Punic Wars / Roman domination		Hebrew lands fall to Romans; Hebrews without homeland until 1948, when Jews given Israel	chaos and unrest	Classic Buddhist Japan	Invasions / Gupta Empire				
500 A.D.				China united	Capital moved to Heian (Kyoto)	First Muslims rule				
1000 A.D.				Sung Dynasty			Maya civilisation in Yucatan	Aztec settlement on Lake islands	Machu Picchu built / Inca civilisation flourishes	
1000 A.D.				Yuan Dynasty / Ming Dynasty		Moghul Empire				
1500 A.D.				Ch'ing Dynasty / Opium War	Civil war			Spanish under Cortes capture Aztec lands	Spanish invasions of Inca and Maya lands	White settlers cultivate Virginia / African Negroes sold as slaves

Columbus reached the New World

Time scale (right margin): 8000 – 7500 – 7000 – 6500 – 6000 – 5500 – 5000 – 4500 – 4000 – 3500 – 3000 – 2500 – 2000 – 1500 – 1000 – 500 – 0 **B.C./A.D.** – 500 – 1000 – 1500 – 2000

The First Africans

The First Africans

Pamela Odijk

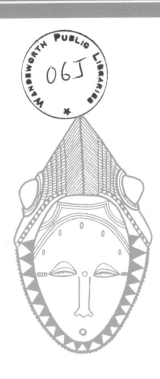

M

The First Africans

Contents

The First Africans: timeline

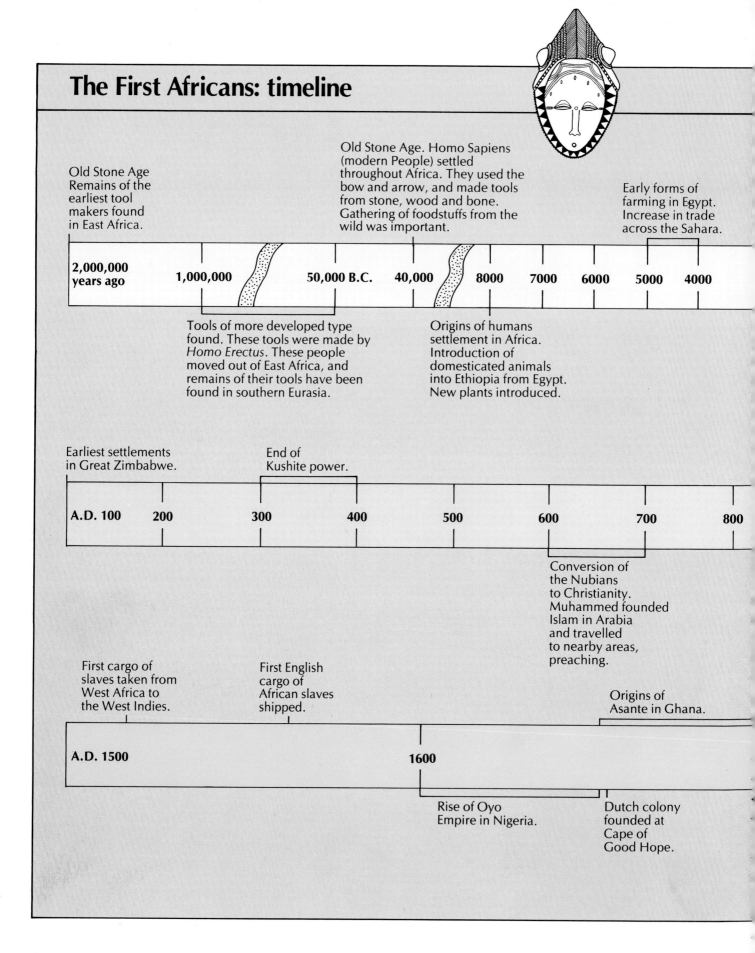

Old Stone Age Remains of the earliest tool makers found in East Africa.

Old Stone Age. Homo Sapiens (modern People) settled throughout Africa. They used the bow and arrow, and made tools from stone, wood and bone. Gathering of foodstuffs from the wild was important.

Early forms of farming in Egypt. Increase in trade across the Sahara.

| 2,000,000 years ago | 1,000,000 | 50,000 B.C. | 40,000 | 8000 | 7000 | 6000 | 5000 | 4000 |

Tools of more developed type found. These tools were made by *Homo Erectus*. These people moved out of East Africa, and remains of their tools have been found in southern Eurasia.

Origins of humans settlement in Africa. Introduction of domesticated animals into Ethiopia from Egypt. New plants introduced.

Earliest settlements in Great Zimbabwe.

End of Kushite power.

| A.D. 100 | 200 | 300 | 400 | 500 | 600 | 700 | 800 |

Conversion of the Nubians to Christianity. Muhammed founded Islam in Arabia and travelled to nearby areas, preaching.

First cargo of slaves taken from West Africa to the West Indies.

First English cargo of African slaves shipped.

Origins of Asante in Ghana.

| A.D. 1500 | 1600 |

Rise of Oyo Empire in Nigeria.

Dutch colony founded at Cape of Good Hope.

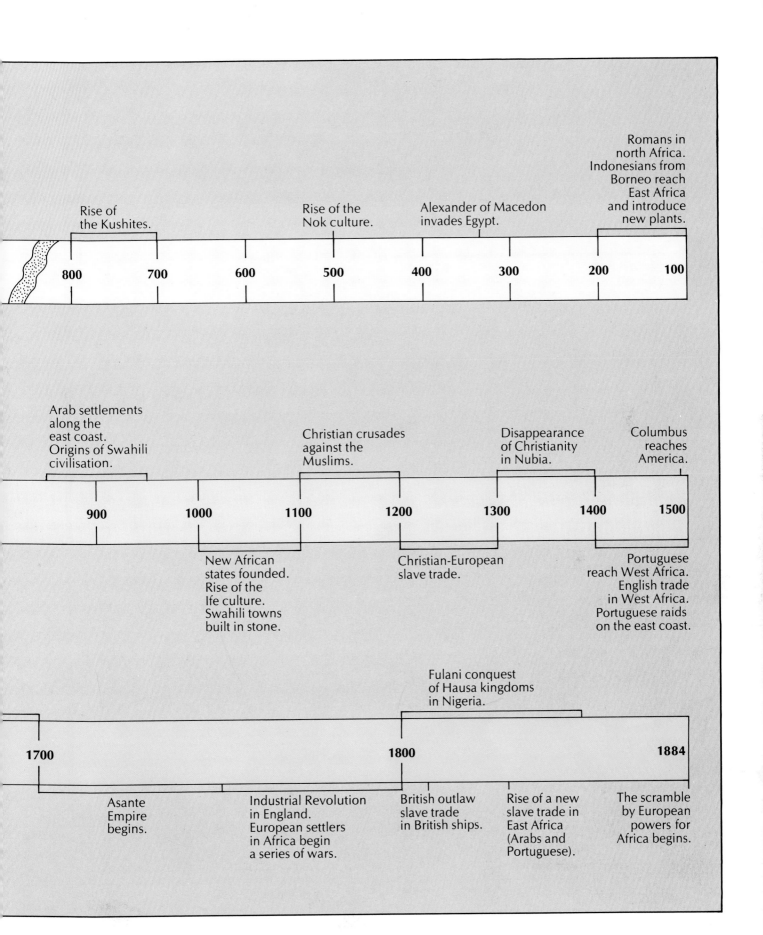

Romans in
north Africa.
Indonesians from
Borneo reach
East Africa
and introduce
new plants.

Rise of
the Kushites.

Rise of the
Nok culture.

Alexander of Macedon
invades Egypt.

800 **700** **600** **500** **400** **300** **200** **100**

Arab settlements
along the
east coast.
Origins of Swahili
civilisation.

Christian crusades
against the
Muslims.

Disappearance
of Christianity
in Nubia.

Columbus
reaches
America.

900 **1000** **1100** **1200** **1300** **1400** **1500**

New African
states founded.
Rise of the
Ife culture.
Swahili towns
built in stone.

Christian-European
slave trade.

Portuguese
reach West Africa.
English trade
in West Africa.
Portuguese raids
on the east coast.

Fulani conquest
of Hausa kingdoms
in Nigeria.

1700 **1800** **1884**

Asante
Empire
begins.

Industrial Revolution
in England.
European settlers
in Africa begin
a series of wars.

British outlaw
slave trade
in British ships.

Rise of a new
slave trade in
East Africa
(Arabs and
Portuguese).

The scramble
by European
powers for
Africa begins.

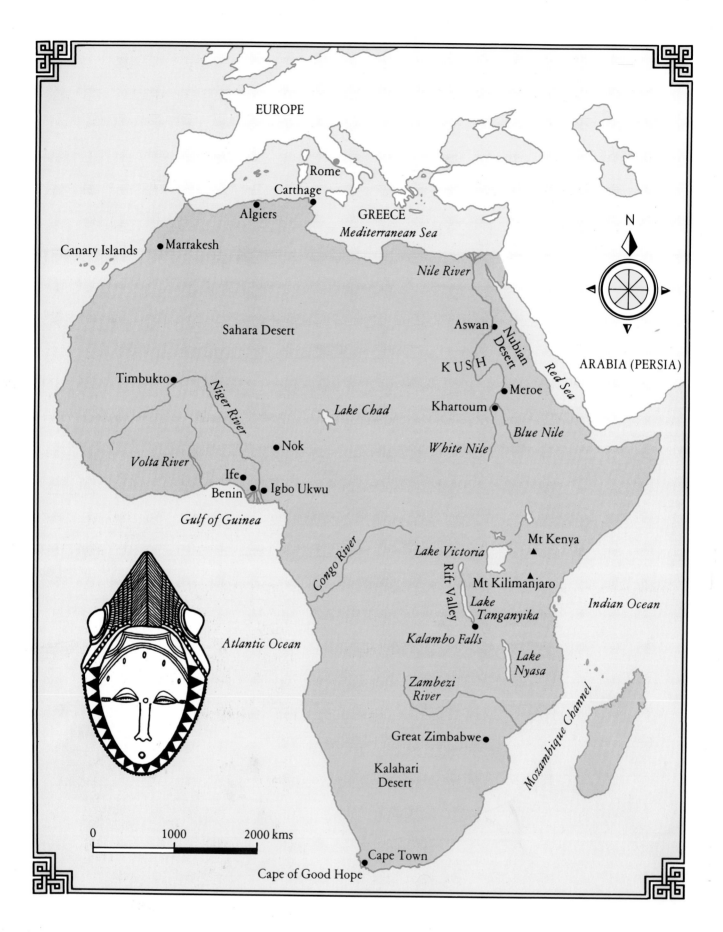

EUROPE

Rome

Carthage

Algiers

GREECE

Mediterranean Sea

Canary Islands

Marrakesh

Nile River

Aswan

Nubian Desert

K U S H

Red Sea

ARABIA (PERSIA)

Sahara Desert

Timbukto

Niger River

Lake Chad

Meroe

Khartoum

Blue Nile

White Nile

Volta River

Nok

Ife

Benin

Igbo Ukwu

Gulf of Guinea

Congo River

Lake Victoria

Mt Kenya

Rift Valley

Mt Kilimanjaro

Indian Ocean

Lake Tanganyika

Kalambo Falls

Lake Nyasa

Atlantic Ocean

Zambezi River

Mozambique Channel

Great Zimbabwe

Kalahari Desert

0   1000   2000 kms

Cape Town

Cape of Good Hope

The First Africans: Introduction

Advanced civilisations have inhabited Africa for thousands of years. **Archaeologists** have found fossil remains so old that the first people in the world may have evolved in Africa. The Greeks knew about Africa for it appeared on Herodotus's world map which he drew in about 450 B.C., and the Greeks called it the land of "the long-lived black peoples" and regarded the African people as being of equal, if not superior, stature to themselves.

Kush was a kingdom established on the Nile in Nubia in about 800 B.C. which ruled all of Egypt for over a century and then withdrew to southern boundaries where it continued as a distinct civilisation until A.D. 300. The Kushites were more progressive than the Egyptians, and developed an iron smelting industry and invented an alphabetic script.

Despite Africa's long history, written historical records about the continent are relatively recent. They are only available for those times and places when literate people were present: either Africans who kept records or foreigners. However, literate records marked an end to Africa's isolation. The first foreigners were the Romans who occupied modern Tunisia in 146 B.C. They were followed by the Arabs, and finally the European travellers, missionaries explorers, pirates and traders. The Arabs called the land *Ifriqiya* and referred to it as "the treacherous land beyond the frontier".

When the Europeans reached Africa in the 16th century the native people were among the most advanced in the world. Some were farmers using iron tools, others had herds of animals, while others had enough skills to live off the land. The people of the northern third of the continent belonged to the urbanised civilisation of Islam. Those in the south were organised into states and communities powerful enough to attempt to defend their lands and trade routes from invaders, but unfortunately not powerful enough to resist the European force and firearms. The Europeans came in search of raw materials and markets essential for their newly industrialised economy, and in search of slaves, and during the 16th, 17th and 18th centuries established slave markets. The Europeans also came to exploit the gold and diamond mines.

Africa suffered the effects of the slave trade with Africans making up the majority of slaves in the Western world. The slave trade continued well into the 19th century, coinciding with the European conquests which began in the 1780s.

By 1884 a scramble for African territory by European powers had begun and resulted in the parcelling up of the whole continent into a bewildering number of European colonial possessions which had a long lasting and damaging effect on the civilisations of old Africa.

This 16th century bronze plaque of two Portuguese was made by the Benin people of Nigeria, West Africa. The Portuguese reached the coast of the Benin kingdom toward the end of the 15th century.

Some Important Events in Africa

When	What Happened
40,000 B.C.	Evolution of Homo Sapiens (modern people) in Africa.
8,000 B.C.	Introduction of domesticated animals into Ethiopia from Egypt. New plants introduced.
5,000–4,000 B.C.	Early forms of farming in Egypt. Increased trade across the Sahara.
800–700 B.C.	Rise of the Kushites.
500 B.C.	Rise of the Nok culture in West Africa.
332 B.C.	Alexander of Macedon invades Egypt. (Greek period.)
200–100 B.C.	Romans in North Africa. Indonesians from Borneo reach East Africa and introduce new plants.
A.D. 100	Earliest settlements in Great Zimbabwe.
300–400	End of Kushite power. Spread of Malaysian plant foods.
850–950	Arab settlements along the east coast. Origins of Swahili civilisation.
1000–1100	New African states founded. Rise of the Ife culture, in West Africa. Swahili towns built in stone.
1100–1200	Christian crusades against the Muslims.
1200–1300	Christian-European slave trade.
1300–1400	Disappearance of Christianity in Nubia. West African gold used to issue European currency. Migrations of Bedoin Arabs into North Africa.
1400–1500	Advances in Zimbabwe culture. Portuguese reach West Africa. English trade in West Africa.
1492	Columbus reaches America.
1400–1500	Portuguese raids on the east coast.
1518	First cargo of slaves taken from West Africa to the West Indies.
1562	First English cargo of African slaves shipped.
1600–1650	Rise of Oyo Empire in Nigeria. Portuguese wars of invasion in Angola.
1650–1700	Origins of Ashante in Ghana.
1652	Dutch colony founded at Cape of Good Hope.
1700–1750	Ashante Empire begins.
1750–1800	Industrial Revolution in England. European settlers in Africa begin a series of wars.
1798	Mungo Park the Scots explorer in Africa.
1800–1850	Fulani conquest of Hausa kingdoms in Nigeria.
1807	British outlaw slave trade in British ships.
1830	Rise of a new slave trade in East Africa (Arabs and Portuguese)
1867	Diamonds found in South Africa.
1884	The scramble by European powers for Africa begins.

Nomadic herding cultures still exist in Africa today. One such culture is the Fulani. This Fulani woman is a high caste woman who carries much of her family's wealth on her. The large rings, which are attached to her hair, are solid gold.

The Importance of Landforms and Climate

The African continent is immense. It is 8,050 kilometres (5,000 miles) long and 7,400 kilometres (4,600 miles) wide at its widest point. The Mediterranean Sea lies to the north, the Atlantic Ocean to the west, and the Red Sea and Indian Ocean to the east. **Volcanic** activity has caused the land to rise and fall, and **fold** and **fault** over millions of years. This activity has produced startling landforms such as the Great Rift Valley which has filled to form Africa's greatest and deepest lakes. Lake Victoria, Africa's largest lake, lies between branches of the Rift Valley.

Victoria Falls on Lake Victoria, Africa's greatest and deepest lake.

Africa has prominent rivers and basins with the Niger, Nile, Volta, Zambezi and Congo Rivers all flowing to the sea, while those around Lakes Chad and the Kalahari have no sea outlets and as such, have formed these lakes. African rivers flow down steep **escarpments** which makes navigation along many of them impossible.

Africa has many high mountains, the highest being Mt Kilimanjaro which rises to 5,895 metres (19,340 feet). There are also low areas such as the Congo Basin and Lake Assal which is 153 metres (502 feet) below sea-level.

In the north lies the great Sahara Desert and in south-west Botswana lies the Kalahari Desert, a sand covered plain lying 915 to 1,830 metres (3,000 to 6,000 feet) above sea-level.

Climate

Many factors affect Africa's climate. Firstly, Africa's position means that much of the continent lies in the tropical zone, thus receiving a tropical climate. Secondly, the position and height of mountain ranges and the plateau block rain bearing winds which blow from the sea. As such, some areas receive a great amount of rain, while others receive less. Also the great width of the land in the north means that rain bearing winds blowing from the sea have little effect, while the narrower land mass of the south receives rain from these winds.

The tropical areas are characterised by hot, wet conditions. The areas near Algiers and Cape Town have a Mediterranean climate. The highland areas have a cool and temperate climate while the highest mountains have permanent ice caps. The desert areas are hot and dry during the day, and very cold at night.

Natural Plants, Animals and Birds

Africa's diversity of landforms and climate has led to a great variety of vegetation, and animal and bird life.

Africa's vegetation ranges from tropical rainforest to desert. In the tropical rainforest (or jungle) there is little undergrowth as the sun never penetrates the canopy (upper layer) of plants and vines. Here grow the broad-leafed evergreen trees, ferns and palms. The savanna consists of grasses, and trees which shed their leaves during the dry season. The savanna extends over most of the continent. The dry lands occur further out in both northerly and southerly directions, extending to the Kalahari Desert and the Sahara. This dry area contains drought resistant plants and shrubs such as the acacia and locust bean, and occasional grass which gives way to thornbush and semi-succulent trees such as the **myrrh** and **boabab**. Forest also covers slopes of the higher mountains.

Africa's exotic flowers, animals and birds were of great interest to the ancient Romans and other European explorers. The animals of Africa created even more interest among the Europeans. Africa's animal life includes monkeys, the rhinoceros (including the rare white rhinoceros), **gnus**, bisons, the hyena, hippopotamuses, elephants, zebras, giraffes and lions, all of which were pursued by Europeans in the interest of science, and for sport and trade. In earlier times, many were shipped back for the unfair gladiatorial combats in Rome, and for private zoos and collections. Birds were caged for the wealthy to own, and animals were slaughtered by the Europeans as a sport using firearms. Trade in skins, furs and ivory led to the exploitation of Africa's animal resources, and the extinction of many animal species.

Africa supports nearly 2,000 different species of birds, including those that are native to Africa and those that migrate there seasonally. Some of the most famous included ostriches, hamerkop and touracos.

Reptiles include lizards, vipers, **elapid snakes** and crocodiles. Also, there are about 2,000 species of freshwater fish, some of which can breathe air and others, like the catfish, can travel overland in wet weather.

Wild zebras roam the grassy plains of Kenya.

Crops, Herds and Hunting

Africa's natural environment determined to a large extent the way the Africans developed and maintained food supplies. People who lived in the grasslands developed different farming activities from those who inhabited the forests and jungles, and those who inhabited the desert fringes were different again.

Agriculture was only possible in Africa during the rainy months. During the dry season, the rapid evaporation of water discouraged the growth of forests and crops. Also, African soils were devoid of **humus** and were highly **leached**.

The art of most West Africans had a spiritual nature. All artworks served a specific and often functional purpose. The object was the bearer of life forces. These Ibo cult figures from Nigeria were connected with yam and taro growing. Such figures were created and respected to ensure a good crop, and to protect it.

Hunters and Gatherers

These were groups who moved quickly around defined areas in search of fish, game, wild edible plants, nuts and berries. Animals were hunted using spears, and bows and arrows. Barbs were used on arrows, spears and harpoons which were used for fishing. Woven nets were an indispensible part of food hunting equipment.

Hunters would burn large tracts of land to drive out various animals. At the edge of forests pits and fall-traps were set to catch the animals as they fled the burning land. Cord stretched across a path at ground level was also used to trip small game and birds.

The hunters and gatherers' diet was supplemented with edible plants and honey which was collected from tall trees.

Shifting Agriculture

Many African tribes practised shifting agriculture. The land was cleared of forest and grass, usually by burning, after which the soil would be turned and crops planted. When the land lost its fertility, usually after several crop harvests, it would be abandoned, and a new area would be cleared. The earliest cereal crops grown were emmer and millet. Many new food crops were introduced to Africa by way of Indonesia and, in later times, the Americas.

Grain crops were harvested, threshed, winnowed and stored. Winnowing was done by throwing the threshed grain in the air so the wind blew the chaff away allowing the grain to fall back to the ground. Woven winnowing baskets were often made specifically for this purpose. Grain was stored in granaries which were built in a similar way to dwellings but were set high off the ground so that rats and termites couldn't get to the grain. Food was regarded as the property of women who were obliged to feed their families from the produce of the land that was cleared and farmed for them.

Crops were endangered by droughts, floods, locusts and birds (especially the quelea finches).

People grew either grain crops, root crops or tree crops, which included oil palms, sesame, bananas, and other fruit, and the **sheabutter tree**.

Nomadic Herdsmen

Nomadic herdsmen were people who were solely dependant on animals and wild plants and grains for food. These people occupied the savanna areas where by moving about, animals could provide abundant food. These nomadic herdsmen did not wander aimlessly: they followed a fixed pattern of routes which took several years to complete. Sometimes the cycle was a seasonal one which took only a year to complete.

In some places people co-operated to carry out both mixed farming (crops and herds). Cattle were the main herd animals, although goats and sheep were also herded. Camel herders lived on the fringes of the desert. Domesticated animals used by the Africans included pigs, sheep and cattle, and were introduced to the continent from Asia by way of Egypt. The exception was the camel which first appeared in Greco-Roman times. African mixed-farmers also kept poultry and pigeons.

The successful raising of cattle was one of the factors which enabled Africans to settle certain parts of the continent that otherwise would not have been possible. The chief enemy of cattle was the **tsetse fly**, but hyenas, lions and other large animals also posed a problem.

Water was always a problem for Africans. Most societies depended on surface supplies or wells as a source of water. However, to wade in a stream to wash or collect water subjected the people to the threat of diseases.

Bronze statue of a hunter made by the Benin people of Nigeria. The hunter's knife is strapped around his chest.

How Families Lived

Many different people inhabited the African continent, with each group making its own adaptations to climate, vegetation and land, and evolving for itself a suitable culture and language. Usually an elder of a large, important family was the head or chief of the group.

Townspeople

Only in one corner of early Africa did food production lead to urbanisation. People moved into the flood plain of middle Egypt in the early 4th millennium and settled in permanent villages. These people also built papyrus boats and developed craft industries such as pottery. People also settled in Kush, an area to the south of Egypt. The Kushites conquered Egypt in the 8th century B.C.

Settled Agricultural People

A woman's day would be taken up with farming duties, grinding meal and cooking. Women were also required to attend to the markets, her children and visit relatives. Women went about their everyday tasks with children tied to their backs and, usually, with containers balanced on their heads.

Men's work was usually seasonal. Their work was heavy work as it involved clearing land. Men's tasks were more varied than the tasks allotted to the women. They were also required to carry out political and legal duties.

Round mud houses from the Mali Empire, North Africa, which became established in the 13th century, and flourished into the 14th century.

Specialised Labour

In some societies people of certain age groups were allocated to traditional jobs such as being porters where there were no beasts of burden. Women were often required to tend to sheep and goats, and milk cows. Other jobs were designated to captives of war or those who were being punished for disobeying tribal laws. There were also jobs which required special skills such as blacksmiths, canoe makers, household keepers, medicine men, and rain-makers. Mask makers were special people who had the necessary knowledge to perform the task of making masks. Slaves had rights, status and conditions of service, and often lived in a household as a member of the family.

Houses

Houses were of various types best suited to the kind of life followed by the community. For more settled communities mud and thatch dwellings made of beams of wood or baked clay were common. Many were circular in shape. They were mostly free standing, though sometimes they were connected by a wall. Typical dwellings of the people in villages in Tanganyika were called *tembe*. These were long rectangular shaped houses with an almost flat roof covered with earth. Houses of some people were constructed of plaited bamboo mats and sun dried brick.

Walls of the mud and thatch huts were often decorated in relief and painted with bright colours. In some cultures, the inside walls of houses were built with huge cavities in which grain was stored, but in most societies grain was stored in special granaries resembling small houses.

The hunters and gatherers and other nomadic people designed houses more appropriate to their lifestyle. Dry season shelters were often little more than windbreaks made from branches and grass. During the wet seasons, domed structures were constructed using branches that were thatched to make them

North African hut built off the ground to make it safe from rats and snakes. Such huts were used to store grain and other foods.

waterproof. Campsites were usually located near lakes and rivers so game coming to drink could be ambushed. People also had ready access to domestic water supplies by setting up lakeside camps.

Marriage

African marriages were usually arranged by parents and people usually accepted their parents' choice of suitable marriage partners. **Bridewealth** (or bride price), was usually a transfer of cattle, goats or other goods to the bride's father and family by the bridegroom and his family.

Although a man was allowed and, in many cases, expected to have more than one wife, each wife and her children usually occupied a separate house.

Food and Medicine

The types of food eaten by a group depended on the area inhabited and the kinds of crops grown or gathered, and the kinds of animals available. The Kalahari bushmen, who lived by hunting and gathering, depended upon certain plant foods for the main part of their diet as well as killing about fifteen to twenty large animals each year. More settled people grew grains and vegetables, and grazed herds of domesticated animals.

Rice was cooked and eaten whole but all other grains were either ground by hand using a grinding stone or pounded in a large mortar. Grains were made into breads, thick porridge, and heavy pancakes. Root crops such as yams could be cooked green, mashed and dried, and finally made into a flour. Oils used in cooking included palm oil, ground-nut (peanut) oil and sesame oil. Sauces and stews were made from meat and vegetables.

Milk and butter were a part of the African diet along with the staple starch crop. Fruit and nuts were a part of the diet when in season.

Medicine

Clean water supplies were often not available and people in early times were powerless against water carrying diseases. Mosquitoes which cause malaria also breed in still water. Life expectancy for most Africans was short.

Medicine was mainly in the control of special priests, medicine men or witch doctors who practised healing by magic and sorcery. Herbs were used and some of these had healing properties. Powerful doctors were also supposed to be able to determine the cause of illness and combat other witches and sorcerers usually by divination and ritual. Frequently ritual dances, costumes and masks were used. Such medicine men underwent long periods of training and guarded their secret knowledge. As with most early civilisations, causes of illness and misfortune were sought and attributed to the spirit world rather than to environmental conditions.

African medicine had a close connection with magic. Attached to this ornament from the Benin people are magical figures, and a bronze medicine bottle.

Ladle made from gourd by the Zulu people.

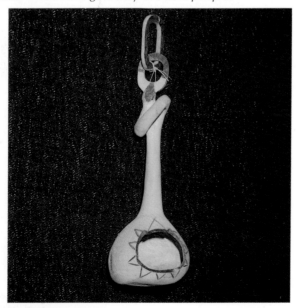

Clothes

In a warm continent like Africa, clothing was worn for personal adornment or as an indication of status, rather than for warmth. Children frequently went naked for the first few years of their life. Adults adopted clothing and ornaments which conformed to the standards of their particular cultural group.

Cotton was grown and spun into cloth. Cloth was also manufactured from bark. Vegetable dyes were used and often, cloth which was manufactured was not only of a very fine quality but also a work of art. Skirts and cloaks were also made from leaves, animal skins and hides.

Personal Ornament

No clear distinction was made between everyday accessories and ritual ornaments. Hairstyles were often a differentiating factor and indicated a person's status. Depending on cultural customs adornments included wooden lip discs, lip rings, earrings, hair rings, plugs, and leg and neck bangles. Tattooing faces and bodies, chipping and filling teeth, and scarring of the body were often used as marks of beautification and as an indication of status with many of these marks being done during initiation ceremonies. Other accessories included combs, headdresses, plaited skullcaps, and even chains and pendants made from plaited yellow straw which was used as imitation gold. Corals were worn by some people.

Royal and Ritual Dress

There were many African kings and their attire was magnificent. Some of the early European travellers recounted tales of African kings and nobles dressed in skins of animals with tassel-tails which trailed along the ground. A Portuguese explorer described a central African monarch as having a pyramid shaped mitre made of brilliant scarlet feathers on his head while around his forehead was a dazzling diadem of various coloured beads. Kings wore symbols of authority and, though they varied from group to group, included jewellery, headdresses, various coloured clothes, ceremonial swords and daggars.

Dancing dress and ritual masks were also of infinite variety and, these too, were dependant on cultural and local customs.

16th century bronze head cast in memory of a Benin queen. The scars on her forehead, often done during ceremonies, were a mark of beauty and status.

Religion and Rituals

There was a great diversity in African religions. Religions of traditional Africa offered explanations of the world and provided instructions on how to behave. Some groups believed in a single creator god, while others believed that there was a pantheon of gods or spirits of ancestors who were in between the people on earth and the ultimate god. Sacrifices and other rituals were used as a means of communicating with the gods. Each cycle of human life was marked by religious ritual as were the seasons.

Wooden staff, carved by a priest, from Yoruba, Nigeria. The staff represents Oshe, god of thunder and lightning, and was used in ceremonies to prevent violent tropical rainstorms.

Religion was the basis for all community life, and religious rituals and beliefs were also ways of passing knowledge on from one generation to another to ensure community survival.

Although there were so many different religions and beliefs, some generalisations can be made about African religions.

There was a general belief in a creator god, a power from where all other powers came, and was often described as "power without beginning". The creator god was not regarded as being either good or evil. This god was neutral and having completed the task of creation, withdrew from the world.

There was also the belief that there were beings or spirits in between god and people and these varied according to custom, but communication was possible through ancestors and in a personal way. These beings were not in themselves worshipped but regarded as helpers or communicators.

It was also believed that once the will of the god was known then the god could be satisfied through rituals such as sacrifices or chanted prayers.

Divination

Diviners read many different signs and omens such as throwing palm nuts and "reading" the pattern where they fell or rubbing an oracle board, or becoming possessed and going into a trance in search of true instructions, or examining the entrails of sacrificed animals. Divination in African religion was very important because it was in this way that instructions about which ritual to perform were given to the individual or the whole community.

When the procedure was known, the correct rituals were performed. It was often only after this that the next step was able to proceed, such as the curing of a patient or deciding a legal matter.

Kingship

In areas where kings and kingships developed, the king and his ancestors were an important part of religious practice. The kingship or the king himself was not permitted to appear to die. This was similar to the practice of the Egyptians.

Rituals

As religious beliefs varied from place to place so did the rituals accompanying these beliefs. Important rituals which involved the whole community were held at prescribed times. Dances and music were used to explain the world and the people's place in it, and gave the people encouragement to go forward and cope with whatever problems might be confronting them.

Dances were performed to play out life on earth or life beyond death.

Masks played an important part in all ritual ceremonies. The mask was used essentially as a form of disguise, so as to conceal the wearer enabling them to enact an existence other than their own. Masks were identified with the god, person or event being re-enacted. Masks were made by special maskmakers according to the secret knowledge and skills of the group. The selection of materials and the making of the mask was as important a part of the ceremony and ritual as the mask itself. Masks were made to invoke terror, respect or humour. They were made for specific purposes such as initiation and funeral ceremonies.

Burial

As with other rituals, burial practices varied from place to place. In some groups the body of the deceased could not be buried until all relatives were certain of the cause of death. This inquiry often took the form of a masked dance. Sculptured figures were often made to house the spirit of the deceased and sometimes funerary figures, which were placed on the tops of graves, represented the deceased or one of the mourners.

"Ring of Silence" cast from bronze by the Senufo people of the Ivory Coast. This is a ritual object connected with initiation ceremonies.

Ceremonial mourning dances were performed in which misery was portrayed by the music and the dance. In many cases the dances continued for days until the people were sure that the soul had progressed along the path to the spirits.

Initiation

At the end of a long period of education and training in traditional ways, rituals were performed in most societies where young men and women were given adult status. As part of the ritual young men and women would be acquainted with their tribal history, lore and traditions.

Marriage

Marriages were made legitimate by the payment of bridewealth. Some societies accepted divorce and some allowed the remarriage of widows. **Ghost marriage** was permitted in some societies whereby a woman could be married to a man already dead in order to raise her children in his name.

Muslims

The first Muslims entered Egypt in A.D. 639 but the main Muslim invasions occurred in two waves: the first, a slow spread from the 7th to the 9th century, and then a second wave beginning in the 13th century. By the 11th century the West African kings and people began to accept Islam, but at the same time, they preserved and revered their native beliefs.

Shrine stool, closely associated with the spirit of the tree, from the Ashanti empire which had its origins in the 17th century. When an Ashanti King died his personal shrine stool was placed on end and returned to the root of the tree, its place of origin and source of spiritual power. Homage is paid to the spirit of the stool and of the tree.

Many Africans were converted to the Muslim faith which effectively stopped the spread of Christianity to these lands.

Christians

As with the Muslim religion, many African people incorporated Christian practices into their lives while at the same time continuing to preserve their native religious beliefs. In later times Christianity gained a larger following.

Obeying the Law

Most African societies governed their people using a form of primitive democracy. Although leadership was a mark of prestige, it did not always ensure total authority, as councils of elders often shared authority and decision making with the leader. Social laws often paralleled family and kin relations, and also ensured that the people lived in a balanced state with their environment to maintain food supplies and thereby guarantee the survival of the group.

All people acquired knowledge which enabled the group to survive and, to safeguard this knowledge, it was put in the form of rituals or laws.

On occasions when the traditional laws were broken, decisions had to be made about the consequences. Tribal courts, often meeting in the open air, made such decisions. The Bantu law courts provided some examples of this.

The Bantu Law Courts

The Bantu law courts were the traditional law courts of the Bantu speaking people. The law court was a group of representatives from all important groups in a community and from them were chosen judges and a provincial chief. The chief and the court sat in a row, arranged in a prescribed order of authority. Those to be heard by the courts appeared before them and were heard. Witnesses were called and also heard. Then the most junior member of the court would offer his opinion, followed by another in order of ascending rank. Finally, the head chief would pronounce final judgement which was binding.

Other communities dealt with problems in similar ways. Societies policed themselves without written laws. Apart from courts, ordeals, seers and diviners were used as a means of deciding outcomes. Ordeals ranged from taking oaths at shrines to taking poisonous substances which were not necessarily lethal.

Influence of Islamic Law

African kings consulted with Muslim rulers about Muslim law especially where it appeared to conflict with the traditional law of the people in a given area. Apart from influencing commerce, Islam affected the African government of cities, states and empires by replacing and dissolving traditional laws and tribal structures and replacing them with Islamic ones.

Influence of the Europeans

As communities grew and changed, so did their laws. With the coming of the Europeans, African people were subjected to many different laws which were imposed on them and, in many cases, must have appeared quite nonsensical to them.

Mask from north-west Africa worn by a priest whenever important decisions or judgements had to be made. It was believed that when the mask, which is female, was worn by a male, it would give him an unprejudiced view and total understanding of all debates.

Writing it Down: Recording Things

Africans had many highly developed languages with some languages containing sounds found nowhere else in the world. The great majority of African languages, though, had no form of writing although various colonial governments and missionaries introduced writing in their languages. Many African languages such as Swahili and Kotoko, the language of the people of Chad, have for centuries been written in Arabic script.

African Scripts

People such as the Vai of Sierra Leone, the Mum of Cameroon, the Tuareg and other Ber-ber groups did have their own script. The Vai and Mum were the only **Negro** tribes to have invented a system of writing. The Vai used a system of 348 signs largely **ideographic** and **pictographic**.

Nubian

From the 8th to the 11th centuries, the Sabean script was used by the Nubian Christians. It was abandoned after the Nubians adopted the Islamic religion and the old form of writing exists only in ancient manuscripts and inscriptions. This writing was not deciphered until 1906. There are instances of Nubian being written in Arabic script.

The Old Nubian script was derived from that of **Coptic**, which was derived from the Greek alphabet with the addition of some Egyptian letters to represent non-Greek sounds.

Ancient rock paintings from northern Africa depicting giraffe and either wild buffalo and antelope or domestic herds. Such rock paintings are a means of passing on information.

Part of a miniature Koran, the Islamic sacred book, from northern Nigeria, dated late 17th or early 18th century.

Meroitic

This was the language of the ancient Sudanese civilisation which existed from 700 B.C. to A.D. 350. Fragments of Meroitic funerary stones show an original alphabet invented and used by the scribes of Kush. Meroitic was written as an alphabet without vowels, and was derived from Egyptian hieroglyphic writing.

The Muslims

From the 11th century onwards many Africans accepted the Muslim faith, and with the new religion came books and learning. Libraries were established, and books were written and published. Histories such as the *tarikhs* or chronicles were written in Timbuktu as were other books of religious and secular interest. Mention is made by travellers in Africa of the profitable trade in books and manuscripts in Timbuktu. Wooden carved parchment boards known as *panka* book covers were often made to protect precious books.

Other Languages and Literacy

With the coming of Europeans to Africa, literacy and learning in other languages was also introduced. Missionaries established schools in Africa during the 19th century and within a short time Africans were editing their own newspapers and making their own translations of Christian works.

Because there was a general lack of written languages, myths, songs of praise and verse were committed to memory and passed on by word of mouth from one generation to another. Many traditional tales found their way in to Western cultures by way of the slave trade. In the courts of African chieftains and kings, professional bards were known to have been given a prominent place. These people were not only praise singers but also the historians of the people.

Legends and Literature

In African legend and literature the greatest form is the dramatic tale. These tales were told and acted out before an audience who participated in the choruses of familiar tales. The storyteller was often supported by a cast of helpers and dancers. Storytellers also created new tales as well as performing traditional ones. Masks were often worn by storytellers and their helpers to re-enact and recreate myths and legends.

Myths and legends were very important as it was in this way that religion, law and history were recorded and told. Being committed to memory, many of the praise songs and tales found their way to the West during the slave trade, where they were overheard and written down as collections of African folktales. These contain examples of the trickster tales and dilemma tales. All African oral traditions had a close link with music. Poetry was meant to be chanted or sung, and much poetry was recited on the **talking drum** rather than spoken or sung. African legends and literature fall into several categories as described in the following.

Wooden dance headdress, from Nigeria, with chameleon on top.

The Creation Stories

These are the most varied and creative. There are many versions of the creation. In some, the original force in the world was death which existed before god. Others show god retreating from worldly cruelty. The creator goddess of the Ijawa people allowed people to choose their own fate in the world, and another creator legend explained deformities in the world as being created by a god who was drunk on palm wine.

In all mythologies, god granted all people eternal life, but god's message was lost or changed, due to the stupidity of the messenger. God is often referred to as *oriki* or *mlenmlen* in praise names. Praise names were also given to chiefs, kings and war leaders.

Poetry

All African poetry was meant to be sung or chanted. There were many forms of poetry, such as oracle verse, hunters' songs, incantations, and magic formulaes. Some traditional poems could take a whole night to recite. Africans used poetry in everyday descriptions of things such as "my bull is dark like a raincloud in a storm".

Folktales

The best known of the African folktales are the animal trickster tales in which the trickster was portrayed as a hare, spider or a tortoise. In these stories, the trickster outwits his opponents. Sometimes the trickster brings about his own undoing such as the story of the tortoise who steals the god's calabash which contains all the wisdom in the world and breaks it in anger when it gets in his way as he tries to scramble over a log.

Another form of the same story is the "escape tale". An example of this is about a cruel king who orders his subjects to build a palace starting from the top and building downwards, otherwise they would be put to death. Eventually the people ask the wise person of the village, who solves the problem. The people finally send a representative to the king to say that they are ready to begin and invite him to perform his traditional role of beginning the building by laying the foundation stone. (The stories of *Brer Rabbit* are examples of African folktales.)

Detail of a painting representing an agricultural fertility dance.

Dilemma Tales

These tales have many possible endings and the audience was asked by the storyteller to provide a suitable one. These closely resembled mystery stories.

How and Why Animal Tales

This is another group of African tales which give fantastic reasons to explain the physical appearance of certain creatures such as "why the tortoise has a broken back".

Proverbs and Riddles

These were a form of popular entertainment where the audience provided known endings and responses. Proverbs also guided the behaviour of people as they were regarded as laws. Some examples are:

"We known whom we love . . ."
(response) "but we don't know who
loves us".
"If a child washes his hands . . ."
(response) "he will eat with kings".

The largest collection of proverbs, some 3,600 in the Tiwi language of Ghana, was collected by a Swiss missionary and published in 1879.

The people of Swahili had a rich literary tradition and, from the 18th century, much of their literature was written in Arabic script. The tales of the Arabian sailors later to be found in *One Thousand and One Nights (Sinbad the Sailor)* found real life counterparts in the people who made their way down the African coast.

In later times many Africans adopted English as a second language and used this language to make their literature available to more people.

Art and Architecture

Art is one way in which original thinking and creative people in a society communicate their ideas, and these ideas can be connected to personal everyday experiences or to religious or political beliefs. African art has its own technique and quality and through European eyes it evokes a sense of mystery. The art of the African people can be understood on three levels:

For its own form and technique
For its purpose and meaning
For its impact on Western art.

The main African art forms which have become widely known outside Africa are sculpture and music.

Bronze head from the Ife culture, Nigeria, made in about the 13th century. Such bronze heads are masterpieces of African sculpture.

African Sculpture and Carving

The earliest surviving African sculptures come from the Nok culture of sub-Saharan Sudan and are dated somewhere in between 400 B.C. and A.D. 200. Nok art was basically pottery and terracotta art.

Other African sculpture and carving were made from materials such as wood and **soapstone**. In the Congo, ivory was a favourite material. Green wood was used for carving and this had to be carefully selected and worked otherwise cracks would appear as it dried. Most work was done first with an **adze**, and the finer work was done with a knife. Sometimes rough leaves were used as sandpaper and carvings were often painted using vegetable dyes and sap from trees. Masks were highly decorated using colours, beads and raffia, as well as other materials.

African sculpture tended to be of three kinds:

The figurine: some figurines were small and simple, while others were used as household gateposts and granary doors. Most were carved from tree trunks and the heaviest weight was at the bottom. Figures were not worshipped but were symbolic. On the Ivory Coast small figurines were used as a place in which spirits of departed ancestors could reside.
The mask: there were three types of masks — those worn over the face, those worn on top of the head, and the "helmet" type mask which was fitted down over the head.
General decoration of objects such as spoons, stools and doors. Most everyday objects were highly decorated.

Bronzes

These were cast using the "lost wax" method. The item was moulded first in clay and covered in wax. This wax would then be modelled. Fine pottery clay was then placed over the wax model and covered again with coarser clay. The mould was then heated to melt the wax which drained out. Molten metal was then poured into the hot mould filling the space left when the wax melted.

The finest surviving bronze sculptures are the bronze heads of Ife in Nigeria which date from the 12th century A.D.

Carved ivory leopard with copper studs worn as an armpiece, probably by royalty (from Benin, Nigeria).

Benin Art

The people of Benin who called themselves Bini had a form of religion in which art had a significant place. The religion respected salvation, safety and fertility, and sacrifices, including human sacrifices, were made at altars. The art was based on the altarpiece heads of cast bronze, each of which supported a carved elephant tusk. Other carved ivory pieces belonging to the _Oba_ or king of Benin have also been found but they were purely decorative. Another form of art was the bronze plaques which were set into mud walls and pillars of houses.

Matting made by the Wogo people, a nomadic culture that lives along the Niger River. Matting was used to erect tents for special occasions such as weddings and religious ceremonies.

African Painting

African painting has a long history. The earliest cave paintings go back thousands of years and their dates still cannot be accurately determined. Some of the earliest paintings were of humans 3½ metres (11 feet) high and animals 8 metres (26 feet) long. Rock paintings have been found in most parts of the African continent.

Some of the most impressive art is shown in the Christian frescoes at Faras which was once a centre for Christian civilisation in the Sudan. Another famous work is a strip painting found in Ethiopia which tells the story of the visit of the Queen of Sheba to King Solomon.

Rock painting and engraving were predominant in the Sahara. Paintings show masks, huntsmen, fishermen, horses and other aspects of the culture of the people who lived there.

Basketry and Leatherwork

Basketry and leatherwork were examples of everyday art. Leatherwork included horse trappings, satchels, bags and clothing. Items of basketry (both everyday items and art objects) were plaited or made using a coiling technique and often had lids. Many were highly decorated with beads, cowrie shells and bright colours. Materials were varied and included twigs, roots, canes and grasses.

30

Architecture

Though the African people generally did not built immense structures, there are some notable exceptions.

At Elephantine Island which was once part of the old Nubian kingdom of Kush, the Pyramid of Meroe shows the location of the royal tombs. Nearby are representations of the gods of the rulers of Kush including the many headed lion god, Apedemak. There are also some stone effigies and engravings of elephants as well as a massive stone enclosure thought to have been used for taming and training elephants.

Relics from other cities such as Kano have been found in the Hausa kingdoms of northern Nigeria. Kano was described by a traveller in 1500 as being "encircled by a wall made of

beams of wood and baked clay."

The Zimbabwes of Africa are of special interest and importance. The word Zimbabwe means "royal court" and there is evidence that over 200 buildings of various royal courts and ruling families were scattered throughout Africa. The most famous is the Great Zimbabwe at Barbosa, thought to have been completed in about A.D. 1300. This stands as a massive walled enclosure built of stones placed on top of each other supported by internal walls. It was once surrounded by other stone structures and mud and thatch dwellings. Another Zimbabwe is Khami in Matabeleland built in the 15th century.

The Swahili Coral buildings are different again. The Swahili were an East Coast trading people, and they built their towns from the rough grey "rag" from the shore of the Indian Ocean. Coral ruins of these old Swahili buildings can still be seen.

Muslim buildings are scattered throughout northern Africa. Ruins of mosques such as the one at Timbuktu, which is the oldest surviving in West Africa, and the great mosque of Jenne, can still be seen.

Shrine in the small town of Kaba Kangaba, on the Upper Niger River, in Mali. Kaba Kangaba was a small kingdom which grew to become the Mali empire in the 13th century. This is the shrine of the Keita clan, which was the clan of the Sundiata, founder of the Mali empire. It is believed this shrine was built in about the 3rd century A.D.

Going Places: Transportation, Exploration and Communication

Africa was known to the Greeks from very early times and the caravan merchants and Berber nomads travelled the northern routes before the 8th and 9th centuries. By the 11th century, the Muslim presence in these lands was making itself felt and following the conversion to their faith of many Africans, a highly profitable book trade was added to the already existing trade.

In the 14th century the Jewish map makers such as Abraham Cresques had drawn atlases of Africa's northern lands. The map routes crossed the Sahara and linked places of wealth and power. Along these routes travelled the camel caravans carrying, among other things, African gold needed for gold currency in Europe. Important trading centres developed at Tahert, Sijilmasa, Marrakesh and Bab al-Zuwaila. By the 16th century the Portuguese had made detailed maps of the African coast.

The Caravans

Along the trade routes, camel caravans going north carrying gold, ivory, ebony and ostrich feathers passed those coming south carrying salt and other scarce and rare items, dates, hides, livestock and dried meats. Berber guides who had known the desert all their lives acted as paid guides, called *takshifs*. Those who became lost in the desert perished from thirst and heat, and casualties were many. The caravan routes declined as ships improved and sea routes were established.

The Slave Trade

Slavery existed in most societies in the world including Africa. Every African trading community had people who were sold as slaves, such as war captives and criminals, who were either put to work locally or sold to the traders from abroad. Before the days of plantations these slaves usually went into domestic or craft services, and male slaves were often given the opportunity to acquire a skill. Sometimes slaves were used as military guards by foreign rulers who thought that these people might be more loyal than their own. Slaves who possessed skills were expensive and usually well cared for. However, even if slaves were well cared for in the early days, they still suffered from home-sickness and isolation once they were taken to another land.

The later slave traders sent out double cargoes: one for buying slaves and one for buying gold. From the business of selling a few slaves in the early years, African kings were gradually pressured into providing more and more. The Portuguese were particularly demanding for slaves.

Brutality in the slave trade grew steadily worse until the value of human life counted for little. Slaves were crammed aboard ships and chained so that even a change of position was impossible. They were sorted on arrival into young and old, fit and weak, diseased and healthy, and ultimately into categories such as "acceptable" and "unacceptable". Slaves were branded with a hot iron, so that they wore a mark of ownership. The anti-slavery campaigners continually pointed out the horrors of the slave trade, usually to no avail, and it continued well into the 19th century.

It has been estimated that some 30,000,000 to 100,000,000 slaves were shipped across the Atlantic to the United States. Slaves from the Arab trade also ran into many millions.

Mopti on the Upper Niger River. Trading centres on the Niger have remained almost unchanged since the days of the earliest explorers. River cities like Mopti, which were also centres for learning and administration, attracted trade from all over the savanna lands to the south, and from the north. Goods were transferred from draught animals to canoes for transport up or down the Niger.

Music, Dancing and Recreation

Traditional African music developed as a unique art form. It had a polyrhythmic structure which means that many simple but different rhythms are played at the same time. The music constantly changed as performers added or improvised on a known theme.

African dancing was part of all religious rituals and the telling and reinforcing of religious myths was done in this way. There were dances for every occasion, from frenzied joyful dancing to sedate dances for funerals. Dancing costumes were as varied as the dances themselves.

African music and dance allowed for great freedom of expression and demanded great skill and precision. However, in some cases the dancer was required to be expressionless and not to appear emotionally involved. At other times dancers were called upon to re-enact other existences, and for this, elaborate masks and headdresses were designed and worn.

Plaque depicting court drummers from Benin, 17th century.

Customs of dancing varied from one community to another, as did musical instruments. Instruments included bells, rattles, zithers, lutes, harps, pipes from reeds, bamboo or animal horn flutes, horns, various kinds of drums and hand claps, all played in various combinations. The **mbiras**, unique to Africa, were an array of metal or fibre reeds, and were played by plucking. In some group dances each dancer selected a drum to dance to and all dancers danced at cross rhythms. The drums also had their own patterns and variations of rhythm. An ending pattern which was recognised brought all drums into a final simultaneous beat.

Christian missionaries disliked the close association of African music and pagan religion and discouraged both music and dance.

African literature was performed as live theatre with the storyteller and supporting "cast". The dramatising of the story and the individuality of the main actor was of great importance. Such literature, had it been written down, would have had a simple plot and could have been told in a few words but its whole impact and dramatic quality would have been lost.

African masks were used as a part of a costume and many African myths were enacted in this way including myths of creation, history and religion. The purpose of the mask was to give a sense of continuity between the present and the past so spectators could become associated with the past through the spirit power of the mask. Spirits depicted in this way were viewed with familiarity and, in some cases, rejoicing, although some masks did represent evil or harmful spirits.

Other Recreations

Puppets representing cult figures have been found and presumed to have been used by professional entertainers.

Bronze horn player from Benin, circa 1500. Music accompanied most ceremonies in West Africa from court rituals to village dances.

Wars and Battles

Some armies of early African kings were large and, by all accounts, magnificent. A 16th century emperor of Kanem-Bornu was said to have equipped his cavalry with golden bits while his hunting dogs had golden chains. The kings of Woloff (in West Africa) had a cavalry of over 10,000 and over 100,000 in the infantry. In later times there is mention of rulers having troops of heavily equipped cavalry which were maintained by the people and always ready to take up arms. Armies of the Hausa kings were professional armies with a cavalry supplied with chain mail, breastplates and shields, quilted horse armour and good weapons.

People fought from behind parapets filled with alternate layers of stone, logs and earth but in later times walls of mud or sun dried brick and masonry were used. At intervals along these walls, towers were constructed from which sentries kept guard, and from where archers fired arrows. Part of an early fortification is still evident at Benin. This fort, though now overgrown with forest, was built by Oba Oguola in the 13th century. It extended around the city for 47 kilometres (28 miles).

The ancient empire of Bornu in central Sudan was a militant state which used heavily armoured and equipped cavalry to defend its empire.

Wars broke out between various groups of Africans as a result of rivalries for wealth and power. In African society the gaining of land and territory was not the purpose of war but rather the gaining of captives (as slaves and subordinates) and cattle. Overpowering a rival gave the victor more wealth. With the coming of the slave trade many African kings went to war with the prime purpose of taking slaves to be sold to the Europeans in exchange for other goods, such as firearms, which only served to continue the problem.

However, there were some people in the Sudan region who were unfamiliar with warfare except for petty raiding and it was these people who suffered greatly in the interests of the slave traders.

16th century bronze plaque from Benin, Nigeria, depicting warrior flanked by attendants, who are shown carrying shields.

Weapons

There were few guns in Africa before 1500 and the first such weapons were cumbersome muzzle loading guns. For most Africans, spears and shields were common weapons, but after the Africans realised that these were powerless against guns, many (such as the Zulu) armed themselves with short stalking knives (*assegi*) and relied instead on surprise raids and close combat where the strength and fitness of the Africans was an advantage. Nets, such as those used to snare and trap animals, were also used in warfare.

War Dances

Flamboyant war dances, such as those performed by the Zulu people, often preceded warfare, and were an essential prelude.

The Africans not only had to contend with intertribal and group rivalries but also with wars against the Europeans, all of whom sent armed forces to Africa. Some of the famous African leaders who resisted European advances (particularly British advances) into Africa were Muhammad Ahmad (of Egypt), Abdelkader (of Western Algeria), King Mesheshwe (of the Basuto), King Prempeh (of the Ashante) and Mahdi (of Eastern Sudan.)

Some of the most bitter fighting took place during the Cape Frontier Wars (often called the Kaffir Wars) from 1779 to 1879. This was a period of one hundred years of intermittent warfare between the colonists and the Xhosa agricultural and pastoral people of South Africa.

Detail of a horse harness from Bornu, in central Sudan. Bornu was a militarist state which relied on heavily armoured cavalry.

African Inventions and Special Skills

Mask Making

Masks were used in African dances and religious ceremonies. They were made by specially trained and initiated mask makers and were often associated with secret cults and societies. An infinite variety of masks existed, all for specific purposes. When masks were not in use they were usually hidden from sight in a special place such as a secret grove.

Wood carvers were highly regarded and vital to the well-being of a community. Without them there would have been no masks and the powers of the spirits could not have been properly invoked, or traditional myths re-enacted.

Iron cast dancing figure from the Mali empire. Clappers are attached to the head, arms and foot.

Iron Smelting

When the Africans embarked on the cultivation of crops, simple stone tools were inadequate, and stronger tools were needed for clearing the forest, and hoeing and harvesting. This led to an interest in metals, particularly iron. From about 500 B.C. the knowledge and mastery of iron smelting had spread throughout the continent. (The source of this knowledge could have been Celtic Europe which was linked to Africa by trade.)

The Sukur people used iron smelting extensively. Their furnaces relied on blasts of air to burn charcoal at a high temperature in a furnace so the iron could be extracted from the ore. Furnaces were built of hard earth and bellows at the base of the furnace provided the "blast". The crude metal was pulled through the same hole as the blast with forceps. This was then pounded and reheated to produce a form of steel which could be made into implements, or traded as a raw material.

As African religion was incorporated into everyday life, these ironsmiths who possessed special knowledge preceded their activities with prescribed rituals which often included a dance. It is thought that the Brazilians learned the skills of iron ore smelting from African slaves.

Polyrhythmic Dancing

This was a unique form of African dancing, which was done to the polyrhythmic structure of African music. Each dancer selected one of the various instrument rhythms and kept their dance to its beat. This meant that dancers were dancing at cross rhythms which gave the dance more dimensions and provided a more spectacular and complete performance.

Zimbabwes

Zimbabwes were royal residences built by kings and ruling families and thought to date from the 13th century. The buildings consisted of massive circular stone walls with stones being placed row upon row forming sound structures without the use of mortar or cement. Although it is thought that over 200 Zimbabwes were built throughout the country, they were not all occupied at the one time. When the surrounding pasture and agricultural land was exhausted, the community moved and rebuilt their huts and a new royal residence.

Great Zimbabwe, built as a residence for a king and his family, from the 13th century.

Agricultural and Hunting Skills

Africans possessed skills of tropical agriculture and hunting based on years of traditional practice. They knew how to live in a balanced state with their environment and were able to farm areas that the Europeans found difficult to cultivate. These appropriate skills were exported to the New World (the Americas) with the slaves in the slave ships.

Textiles

Textiles, especially those of West Africa, were superior both in design and quality to those of the European world. The technique of fast-dyeing cottons as practised by the Africans was far superior.

Why the Civilisation Declined

Any intrusion into a culture or civilisation tends to disrupt it. Muslims and Christians entered Africa and undermined and altered the traditional religions and belief systems of the people. However, this was not completely disruptive as the Africans learned to assimilate both these religions into their indigenous culture. The greatest disruption to African civilisations was the intrusion of Europeans who came as explorers, traders, slavers, looters, plunderers, colonisers and arms traders.

Some early Christian missionaries did have an insight into what was happening to African civilisations. Bishop William Tozer understood when he wrote:

"... What do we mean when we say that England or France are civilised countries and that the greater part of Africa is uncivilised? Surely the mere enjoyment of such things as railways and telegraphs and the like do not necessarily prove their possessors to be in the first rank of civilised nations... Nothing can be so false as to suppose that the outward circumstances of a people is the measure either of its barbarism or its civilisation..."

The slave trade helped speed up the decline of African civilisation. The earlier slave trade, bad as it was, was not as disastrous as the slave trade of the 17th century when shiploads of helpless Africans were forced aboard ships and then forced to work on the plantations in the New World.

European explorers pushed their way into African lands and by 1884, had begun a scramble for African colonies and lands. By 1914 the colonisation of Africa was complete.

With the coming of the European colonies came the establishment of cities, railways, plantations and cash crop agriculture. The black populations moved away from many of their traditional areas and were absorbed by these new entities. As a result the people learned to work, first as slaves and, later, for white people's wages. They were eventually forced to accept and understand the significance of money and Western goods. People needed to have money to pay taxes and fines, and to buy clothing and other goods which they could no

Young Ibo boy from Nigeria. The Ibo lived in the dense African forest where they farmed land, raised animals and gathered materials from the wild. Small boys gathered useful produce from the forest. The Ibo still lead their traditional lifestyle in Africa today, though many Ibo have gone to the cities to work, and to other countries such as Britain to study.

longer provide for themselves as their lands had been forcibly taken from them. Money even became a substitute for traditional wealth to pay bridewealth and to obtain cattle. Also economic development of the Western kind placed great strains on kinship and inheritance systems. White influence dominated and destroyed the highly advanced civilisations of Africa with scant regard for what was being replaced.

Today, although many African people have won independence their economies have been depleted of major resources. Where independence has not been won, like in South Africa, the whites have turned blacks against each other.

Many European ways were featured in African art. This wooden carving from the Lower Congo shows a European being carried in a hammock by two Africans.

Glossary

Adze A heavy chisel-like tool fastened to a wooden handle. It was often used to shape timber.

Archaeologist Person who studies a particular culture, usually prehistoric, by excavating artefacts.

Ashanti An agricultural people of Africa who lived originally in the Ashanti region of Ghana.

Balsa raft Rafts made from the balsa tree or corkwood tree, native to tropical Africa. The wood is very light.

Bantu The principal linguistic family of Africa. These languages are spoken from the equator to South Africa and include Swahili, Tswana, Zulu, Ganda and Congo and refer to the Negroid people who speak these languages.

Basuto (Sotho or Suto) A linguistic and cultural group of Africa. The language is a Bantu language. Most Basuto groups rely on cultivation and the herding of animals.

Berber A people of North Africa. They retained their original culture until the Arab invasions of the 12th century. When the Berber peasant economy was disrupted they assumed a nomadic life instead. Many became Muslims.

Boabab tree A large thick trunked tree native to tropical Africa (and Northern Australia). The woody fruit of this tree contains a tasty pulp. The fibre from the bark was used to make rope and cloth. The trunks were often used as water containers or shelters.

Bridewealth (or bride price) A price paid by the groom and his family to the bride's father and family in order to marry. The payment was usually made in the transfer of cattle, goats, barkcloth, foodstuffs, axes, spears and iron tools. A poor man who had few possessions may have been allowed to pay bridewealth in terms of servitude and labour to the bride's family. If divorce was permitted, the bridewealth often had to be repaid.

Calabash A container made from a hollowed out gourd and often used to carry water. It was also used as a bowl or basin.

Caravan A group of merchants or others travelling together for safety through the desert or other areas. Caravans using camels as pack animals crossed the trade routes of Africa's north and the Sahara.

Cassava (or manioc) A tuberous plant cultivated in the tropics for food. From this root a cassava flour could be made.

Coptic The now extinct language of Egypt which developed from ancient Egyptian.

Dohw A one or two masted sailing vessel with slanting triangular sails. Swahili sailors learned many of their sailing and navigating skills from the Chinese.

Dilemma Tales A form of African short story which allows the audience to speculate as to the correct ending. An example is the story of a boy who must choose between his father who is a cruel and unjust man, and a kind foster father who brought him up.

Elapid snakes Snakes which have fangs at the front of the upper jaw. The African species includes the highly venomous mambas. Its bite causes an almost certain death.

Escarpment A long cliff like ridge of rock caused by faulting or fracturing of the earth's crust.

Fall-traps A pit camouflaged by branches and grass into which an animal falls when chased. It can also refer to hidden trip lines stretched between trees designed to make pursued animals fall so they can be killed.

Fault A fracture in the rocks of the earth's crust.

Fold A bending of the earth's crust caused by volcanic activity.

Gerbil (or sand rat) One of the many burrowing rodents found in Africa [and Asia]. They generally live in dry sandy areas but also in grasslands and cultivated fields.

Grubbing stick A stick used to uproot the soil or plants from the soil.

Humus Organic matter in the soil derived from decomposing plant and animal substances. As humus decomposes, these substances change into forms usable by plants.

Kafir potato (or Coleus) A vegetable common in southern Sudan and surrounding areas that was later introduced to India.

Leaching The loss of fertile substances washed out from the top layer of soil. The rate of leaching increases with heavy rainfall, and high temperatures, and with the removal of protective vegetation.

Maize A grain bearing plant which grows its pale yellow grain in large ears or spikes.

Mbira An African musical instrument consisting of a series of tuned metal bamboo tongues attached at one end to a soundbox that has a resonator. A mbira is played by holding the instrument in the hands and plucking the strings with the thumbs and forefingers.

Meroitic language This was the language spoken in the ancient city of Meroe in present day Sudan. From 200 B.C. to the 4th century A.D. Meroitic inscriptions were written in two types of script, and in hieroglyphic script for inscriptions. Meroitic funerary inscriptions survive as do some papyrus fragments. The language is still mostly undeciphered.

Muslim One who follows the religion and law of Islam which is based on the teachings of the prophet Mahammed.

Myrrh tree (commiphora) An incense tree from which a bitter tasting coloured gum is obtained. It was used in perfumes, cosmetics and medicines.

Negro A person of black African ancestry.

Praise Names These were names given to gods, people and plants which described their praiseworthy qualities. Professional bards were both praise singers and historians who chanted praise names. The praise name was the most important form of oral literature.

Pygmy A term applied to some groups of African people who are of short stature. Most pygmies live in tropical Africa.

Sheabutter tree (or shea tree) An African native tree, the nuts of which are collected. It grows in a semi-wild state and is only occasionally cultivated. It provided an important source of fat which was not used for eating but for cosmetic purposes.

Soapstone A soft mineral which has a soapy greasy feel which gives it its name. It was used for carvings, ornaments and utensils.

Talking Drum A popular term for various drums which are played in such a way as to imitate or simulate language. They are used for communication.

Trickster Tales A type of African folktale in which an animal hero uses cunning to outwit a bigger and stronger opponent. Some African tales have human tricksters.

Tsetse fly A bloodsucking fly which attacks animals and humans, and causes a sleeping sickness in humans, and a disease called nagana in cattle. The flies attack during the warmest part of the day.

Volcanic The result of the activity of volcanoes in early times.

Witch Doctor (or medicine man) A person said to possess mystical powers so as to be able to detect witches and sorcerers and combat their evil actions and intentions. This was done by divination. These people acted on behalf of individuals, and groups of communities. Underlying their practice was the widespread belief that everything in the world was controlled by supernatural forces.

Zimbabwe Historical stone buildings, the largest of which was called the Great Zimbabwe near modern Fort Victoria. This ruin was once a political centre as well as a trading centre.

Zulu An African Nguni-speaking cultural group who were traditionally grain farmers who also kept herds of cattle. They were displaced from their lands by invading Europeans during many years of warfare in the 19th century.

The Africans: Some Famous People and Places

King Mesheshwe (Mshweshwe, Moshoeshoe, Moshesh)

King Mesheshwe was the first chief of the Sotho (Basuto) nation which he founded. He was born about 1786 and died in 1870. He gained a reputation for leadership and daring early in his life by conducting successful cattle raids. (His name, Mesheshwe is supposed to be an imitation of the sound made by a knife when shaving.)

He united various small groups into the Sotho or Basuto nation, which Europeans called Basutoland, which he ruled from Thaba Bosiu (Mountain of the Night). Although he allowed French missionaries to preach among his people, he supported the native religious customs and only became a Christian on his death bed. He sought advice from the missionaries as to how to deal with other Europeans.

In 1843 he accepted the British as allies (against the Boers) but within five years Mesheshwe's lands were annexed by Britain. Disputes followed and the British were defeated. However, the British again annexed Basutoland in 1868.

Al-Mahdī

Muhammad Ahmad, known as al-Mahdī or the "Divinely Guided One" created an Islamic state which reached from the Red Sea to Central Africa. He was born in 1844 and became absorbed in Islamic religious study when he was a student at Khartoum.

In 1881 he believed that god had appointed him to purify Islam and to destroy all who opposed it. He gained many followers over the next few years and in 1883 defeated three large Egyptian armies. In 1885 he captured Khartoum from the British.

He set up his capital at Omdurman on the left bank of the Nile and directed his empire from there. He became ill, probably from typhus, soon after and died there on 22 June 1885, at the age of 41.

Although British historians described him as a wicked person, a false prophet and an ogre, he was a brave and brilliant leader who played an important part in African history.

Dr David Livingstone

David Livingstone was a Scotsman, born in 1813, who changed people's attitudes toward Africa and the Africans. He became a missionary in 1840 and went to Africa, leaving his wife and children, and spent the next fifteen years there as an explorer. By 1853 he undertook a major expedition into central Africa. During this expedition he discovered and named the Victoria Falls. When he returned to Britain in 1856 he was hailed as a hero.

In 1866 he set out in search of the source of the Nile. People became concerned about him when members of his expedition returned to Zanzibar and reported his death.

A newspaper correspondent, Henry Morton Stanley was sent by his publisher to find David Livingstone, which he did in 1871. Stanley joined Livingstone in further explorations but finally left Africa in 1872 while Livingstone remained behind.

Livingstone continued his quest for the Nile but died in the attempt in 1873. His heart was removed and buried in African soil while his body was taken back to England for burial at Westminster Abbey in 1874.

Kingdom of Benin

This was one of the main West African kingdoms founded before A.D. 1300 by the Edo people and reached its peak during the 14th and 17th centuries. It was famous for its kings, called *obas*, the most famous of whom was Ewuara the Great who ruled from about 1440 to 1480. His son Ozolua who ruled from 1480 to 1504 was also a great oba.

Benin was a trade centre where trade in ivory, pepper, palm oil and slaves flourished but this declined in the 19th century. By 1897 the old kingdom of Benin was incorporated into British Nigeria.

Ife

Ife, formerly called Ile-Ife, is one of the oldest towns of the Yoruba people. It was thought to be the birth place of the human race by the Yoruba and to have been founded by the son of the god Oduduwa. It was the capital of an old kingdom and probably named after Ifa, the god of divination.

It is famous for its terracotta sculptures and bronzes. The famous bronze castings were made known to the European world in 1910 by a German explorer and archaeologist, Leo Frobenius.

Abdelkader

Abdelkader, whose full name was Abd al-Qādir Ibn Muhyī ad-Dīn Mustafā al-Hasani Al-Jazā'ira, was an Algerian (born in 1808) who led his people against the French invasion of his territory. The Treaty of Tafna in 1837 ended the conflict and gave Abdelkadar limited power. He was able to extend his power and control as far as the Moroccan border.

The agreement with the French broke down and further struggles followed from 1840 to 1846. The French were led by General T.R. Bugeaud who defeated and imprisoned Abdelkadar. He was freed in 1852 after which he lived in Damascus.

Abdelkadar was been described as being a handsome and intelligent man, and a brilliant leader. He was a religious and educated man who spoke well, wrote poetry and lived a very simple life in a tent.

Mungo Park

Mungo Park was a Scotsman (born 1903) who was asked by the African Association to explore the course of the Niger River. He began his expedition at the mouth of the Gambia River in 1795. During the course of his explorations he became ill, was imprisoned by the Arabs, escaped, and continued his journey with only a horse and a compass. He finally reached Pisania after being helped by a slave trader. He published a book called *Travels in the Interior Districts of Africa*, following this expedition. In 1805 he led a second expedition along the Niger but this party was attacked and Park drowned.

The Ashanti Empire

This empire extended from the Komoe River to the Togo Mountains in what is now southern Ghana. Their most famous leader was probably Osei Tutu whose capital was at Kumasi. His authority was symbolised by the Golden Stool (*sika 'dwa*) upon which all kings were enthroned.

Slaves were supplied by the Ashanti to the British and Dutch traders during the 18th century. In return the Ashanti were given firearms which enabled them to increase their territory.

Osei Tutu died in about 1717 and a period of war followed until a new leader emerged, Opoku Ware, who ruled from 1720 to 1750. Under his leadership the Ashanti conquered more territory. He was followed by Osei Kwadwo (ruled 1764–77), Osei Kwame (who ruled from 1777–1801) and Osei Bonsu (1801–24).

In 1807 the British outlawed the slave trade. The Ashanti defeated a British fighting force in 1824 but peace was established by 1831. By 1863 under leader Kwaku Dua, the Ashanti were again warring with Britain whose forces were led by Sir Garnet Wolseley. By 1874 the Ashanti lands were in British control and the Ashanti leader King Kofi Karikari was deposed and succeeded by Mensa Bonsu. By 1902, the Ashanti lands were declared a British crown colony and the Ashanti leader Prempeh I ceded his power to the British.

Index

Acknowledgements

The author and publishers are grateful to the following for permission to reproduce copyright photographs and prints:

Australasian Nature Transparencies: (NHPA) p.13, (P. Jeans) p.24; Ronald Sheridan/The Ancient Art and Architecture Collection: cover, pp.12, 14, 15, 18, left, 36; Werner Forman Archive pp.9, 11, 16, 17, 18 right, 19, 20, 21, 22, 23, 25, 26, 27, 28, 29, 30, 31, 33, 34, 35, 37, 38, 39, 40, 41.

While every care has been taken to trace and acknowledge copyright, the publishers tender their apologies for any accidental infringement where copyright has proved untraceable. They would be pleased to come to a suitable arrangement with the rightful owner in each case.

Cover design, maps and art: Stephen Pascoe

First published 1989 by
THE MACMILLAN COMPANY OF AUSTRALIA PTY LTD
107 Moray Street, South Melbourne 3205
6 Clarke Street, Crows Nest 2065

Associated companies and representatives throughout the world.

National Library of Australia cataloguing in publication data.

Odijk, Pamela, 1942–
   The first Africans.

   Includes index.
   ISBN 0 333 47779 0.

   1. Africa — History — To 1498 — Juvenile literature. I. Title. (Series : Odijk, Pamela, 1942–   . Ancient world).

960'.1

Set in Optima by Setrite Typesetters, Hong Kong
Printed in Hong Kong

Oceania | Europe | Africa

	Australian Aborigines	Maori	Melanesians	Greeks	Romans	Angles, Saxons & Jutes	Britons	Vikings	Egyptians	First Africans
	c50 000 B.C. Aborigines inhabit continent									40 000 Evolution of man
8000	Torres and Bass Straits under water							The Baltic — freshwater lake		Farm settlements
7500										
7000	Lake Nitchie settled			Neolithic Age						
6500				Settled agriculture						
6000										
5500										
5000	South Australian settlements								Egypt-early farms	Increased trade across Sahara
4500										
4000							Hunting and gathering			
3500	Ord Valley settlement								Predynastic	
3000				Bronze Age				The first farmers		
2500				Crete — palaces					Old Kingdom / Giza pyramids	
2000				Mainland building			Megalithic monuments raised		Middle Kingdom	Sahara becomes desert
1500								Bronze Age	New Kingdom	
1000				Dark Age			Farms and buildings established		New Kingdom declines	Kushites
500				Colonisation / City-states established / Classical Age / Wars — lands extended	Rome found / Republic established / Rome expands through Italy and foreign lands		Ogham alphabet in use	Celtic Iron Age / Roman Iron Age	Persian conquest / Greek conquest / Roman rule	Nok / Greek influence
B.C. / A.D.		Legend: Kupe found New Zealand and told people how to reach there		Hellenistic Age / Empire divided, lands lost. Culture enters new phase	Empire begins: Augustus — emperor / End of Western Roman Empire	Hengist and Horsa arrived in Kent / England: 12 kingdoms / Athelstan rules all England / Norman Conquest	Roman invasion / Britain becomes two provinces / Saxons settle	Vendel period / Army invade England / Christianity adopted / Viking laws recorded		Kushites' power ends / Arabs settle east coast / Christian European slave trade
1500	Dutch explorers sight Aborigines	Maori arrive / Great Britain annexed New Zealand	Europeans dominate / Cook's voyages / Christianity is introduced							Europeans divide Africa
2000	First White settlers									